Thoughts and Feelings by Norma

NORMA HARRISON

BALBOA.
PRESS

A DIVISION OF HAY HOUSE

Balboa Press books may be ordered through booksellers or by contacting:
Balboa Press
A Division of Hay House
1663 Liberty Drive
Bloomington, IN 47403
www.balboapress.com
1 (877) 407-4847

Because of the dynamic nature of the Internet, any web addresses or
links contained in this book may have changed since publication and
may no longer be valid. The views expressed in this work are solely those
of the author and do not necessarily reflect the views of the publisher,
and the publisher hereby disclaims any responsibility for them.

The author of this book does not dispense medical advice or prescribe
the use of any technique as a form of treatment for physical, emotional,
or medical problems without the advice of a physician, either directly
or indirectly. The intent of the author is only to offer information
of a general nature to help you in your quest for emotional and
spiritual well-being. In the event you use any of the information in
this book for yourself, which is your constitutional right, the author
and the publisher assume no responsibility for your actions.

Any people depicted in stock imagery provided by Thinkstock are
models, and such images are being used for illustrative purposes only.
Certain stock imagery © Thinkstock.

Printed in the United States of America.

ISBN: 978-1-4525-2089-6 (sc)
ISBN: 978-1-4525-2090-2 (e)

Library of Congress Control Number: 2014915167

Balboa Press rev. date: 10/09/2014

To a higher being of your choice.

Thanks to Jack and Paula LaRue
also to Rose Johnson

To you as you read these poems
may you find the comfort and the
joy as I did as I wrote them.

To My Mother

Would you love me if you weren't my
mother?
Could you love me as a friend?
If tomorrow, we met as strangers,
would our friendship just begin?
If somehow we met in passing,
Would I know you? Or, would you
know me?
Or do we see each other through eyes
that only see?
Oh, you are the mother.
And, the daughter just happened to be
me.
If somehow I have failed you,
I pray to make amends.
Oh, I'm proud to be your daughter.
I'd like to be your friend.
How much I've taken for granted.
How much I've failed to see.
That you're not just my mother
but what a friend you are to me.

THE "CARPENTER'S" LADDER

YOU PLACE THIS LADDER IN MY
  SIGHT
AND BID ME--START THE
  CLIMB!
WITH TOOLS OF GOD IN MY
  HEART
THE FIRST RUNG IS MY MIND.

DEEP IN THOUGHT AND WITH
  LOVE OF GOD,
THIS LADDER IS MY LIFE.
THE FIRST STEP I HAVE TAKEN,
THE SECOND IS MY STRIFE.

I USE THE TOOLS THAT GOD
  HAS GIVEN,
TO GUIDE ME ON MY WAY.
HIS GUIDING LIGHT IS MY BEAM
THAT GUIDES ME DAY BY DAY.

THE SECOND RUNG LIFTS ME
    UP
AND GIVES ME STRENGTH TO
    CLIMB,
WITH JOY OF HEART AND
    PEACE OF MIND,
MY JOURNEY IS SUBLIME!

THIS LADDER IS A LARGE ONE.
THERE IS PLENTY OF ROOM
    FOR ALL:
THE RUNGS ARE STRONG AND
    STURDY,
THERE IS NO NEED TO FALL.

WHERE DOES THIS LADDER
    LEAD TO?
THAT IS PURELY UP TO YOU.

IT GOES AS FAR AS YOU CAN
CLIMB,
BUT THERE IS MUCH FOR YOU
TO DO.

CHRIST IS RIGHT BEHIND YOU,
AND THAT YOU SURELY KNOW.
AS THE LOAD OF LIFE IS
LIGHTER,
AND YOUR AURA--A GLEAMING
GLOW.

THIS LADDER LEADS TO
HEAVEN, AND TO THE SIDE
OF GOD--
THE RIGHT TO LIVE IN
PARADISE,
WHERE THE "6" OF MAN, PLUS "1"
MAKE THE HOLY NUMBER "7".

HAPPY BIRTHDAY, MOMMA

THIS COMES RIGHT FROM MY
   HEART
IF WE COULD SHARE OUR
   FEELINGS
WHERE WOULD WE START?

SOMETIMES WORDS JUST GET
   IN THE WAY
WHEN THOUGHTS AND
   FEELINGS
ARE WRAPPED IN LOVE--
WHAT DOES ONE SAY?

MY LOVE IS ENTWINED SO
   MUCH
WITH THE LOVE THAT DWELLS
   WITHIN YOUR HEART.
WITH THE LOVE NEVER ENDS-
BUT WHERE DOES LOVE START?

LOVE MUST BE ETERNAL--
A NEVER ENDING RING.
GOD IS LOVE:
LOVE IS A BEAUTIFUL THING!

Say "I Love You"

How long has it been since someone
   said, "I love you"?
Not "I love you" in a passionate sort
   of way,
But "I love you" in a Christian
   loving way.

How long has it been since someone
   held you in their arms?
Not to feel the nearness of your body,
but to hold your loving charms?

The graying of your hair and the
   deepness in your eyes
hold the magic and the mystic secret
of the beauty in the skies.

The lonely time we spend wondering
What life is really all about.

When all the time, we fail to look
    inside---
we only see--what's out!

How long has it been since you said "I
    love you"?
Say it to someone soon--They will say,
    "I love you too"
Take some loving soul and hold them in
    your arms.
Feel the warmth that swells within,
and the joy---now that is charm!

Love must be kept alive and to do it,
We must try to say "I Love You".
Isn't that better than, a cold, impersonal,
    "good bye"?

The Wonders of God's Creation

Does a tree feel the admiration of
   your eyes?
Have you noticed how clouds
   respond
when you look up at the sky?

The colors of the rainbow are
   admired by all.
What a picture!
The leaves on the trees –in the Fall!

Each sunset is different–what a show!
It is all yours to admire (this you
   know)

The list is endless and right at hand
Yours to appreciate and this
   you can.

The brook sings and babbles
As it flows on by.
It even enjoys the reflection of
the sky!

The scales on a fish, so perfect in
line,
The motion of a breeze- so
sublime!

The birds sing their praises of their
own kind,
dressed in fine feathers and plume.

We walk on the grass that is so
green.
Each day the scene is different that
We've ever seen.

A Garden Of Eden for Adam
  and Eve?
This was all meant for you and me!
And this I believe.

I look at God's wonders,
Feeling naked and free–
God created all of this-------
Then He created---------Me!!!

August 30, 1978

I came into this world
so naked and without name.
Who knows the secrets that I hold
or from where I really came?

So dependent upon my mother
Or surely, I would die.
The only language known to me
is to laugh, or to cry.

My soul is deeply buried
Its mysteries to unfold.

I must learn to walk alone
and to do what I am told.

Then comes the day when I decide
this life is <u>mine</u>, to say,
what clothes I'll wear,
the company I keep, or
how I choose to pray.

WHO AM I

UNDERSTAND ME FOR
   WONDERING,
"WHO I AM", OR WHAT I OUGHT
   TO BE.
BUT MAKE ME AWARE OF WHAT
   I AM
AND WHAT I MAKE OF ME.

THERE IS A REASON FOR "WHO
   I AM",
FOR THAT IS GOD'S PLAN
   FOR ME.
FOR WHAT I AM IS UP TO ME,
AND WHAT I BECOME TO BE.

I'VE HAD MY CHANCE IN LIVES
   BEFORE
AND FELL SHORT ALONG
   THE WAY.

THAT'S WHY "I AM WHO I AM";
THAT'S WHY I LIVE TODAY.

FOR MY SHORTCOMINGS OF
  YESTERDAY,
THE MISTAKES ALONG THE WAY,
AND THE THINGS THAT CAN'T
  BE CHANGED,
I MUST PAY FOR--TODAY.

IF GOD CHOOSES IN HIS PLANS,
TO HAVE ME LIVE AGAIN,
I ASK GOD'S BLESSINGS IN THIS
  LIFE
AND TO FORGIVE ME OF MY
  SINS.

THEN SOMEDAY WHEN I
  RETURN,
AND WONDER "WHO I AM",
AND WHAT I MADE OF ME,
I'LL BE A BETTER PERSON THAN
  I AM TODAY
AND OF WHAT I SEE IN ME.

AND IF, IN THIS LIFE, I REACH
  THIS GOAL,
TO BE BETTER THAN THE LAST,
MY FUTURE LIFE WILL BE THE
  GREATEST;
SO MUCH BETTER THAN THE
  LAST!

There Is Glory In Heaven

There is glory in Heaven,
There is glory in your resting place.
One day, I'll meet you there.
We will dance to the glory
and sing such happy songs.
Oh! Won't we be a happy pair!

We'll don our Angel's wings,
and let our halos shine.
The trumpets will blow to tell the heavens
that I am yours and that you are mine.

We'll send our children to Cherub school
where learning is such fun.
They will learn of all the goodness
and sing the songs that we have sung.

Happiness is the way of life,
no sadness in the air.

Golden sunshine lights the day,
there are birds and flowers everywhere.

Where water flows like crystals and
flows down upon the earth,
to nourish all of the people and
send messages of our new birth.

So let the trumpets blast,
beautiful songs of love,
to announce that we have moved
from life on earth and
dwell in the heavens above.

NOT MY WILL, BUT
THINE BE DONE

OH, MY GOD, PLEASE TELL
  ME WHY,
ON SUCH A BEAUTIFUL DAY,
MY HEART BREAKS AND BIDS
  ME-- "CRY?"

I LOOK BACK AND COUNT MY
  BLESSINGS--
THEY PILE SO HIGH, THEY ALL
  BUT TUMBLE.
AND LEAVE ME SO CONFUSED
  THAT IN MY
OWN BLESSINGS--
I FALL AND STUMBLE.

MY LONELINESS IS BEYOND MY
  STRENGTH,
AND EVEN ON THIS SUNNY DAY

MY WEAKNESS IS MY WEAKEST
  LINK.

GIVE ME STRENGTH, DEAR
  GOD, I PRAY.
GIVE ME STRENGTH,
  DEAR GOD,
TO RISE WITH THE RISING SUN
AND DRY MY TEARS AND TO
  REALIZE
THAT MY NEW LIFE HAS JUST
  BEGUN!

MY FAITH IS STRONG AND MY
  COURAGE
IS IN THE SHADOW OF THE SUN.
I PRAY, DEAR GOD, LET THE
  SUN SHINE

ON MY DEEPEST SHADOW AND
ASSURE ME--
NOT MY WILL--BUT THINE BE
DONE! AMEN.

How Cancer Changed My Life

The tragedy of cancer hit my family. There were just two members in our family. My husband and myself.

We fought this battle together and we were not one of the fortunate ones who won.

My darling husband died after a courageous battle that only he could tell you about, and that story can never be told.

When he died a part of me died also. This is now my battle, as there is still life in me that cries to go on.

Now my battle starts. With courage, faith and strength from God. I must pick up the broken pieces and find new growth, a meaning for new life.

There is constant death among everything living and also new growth.

With the strength, courage, faith and hope that God provides, I look for the new buds of life forming on my new branches of life which shall take on the pattern of a new life, and I too shall go on with meaning and a purpose in my life.

The beauty and love that existed when my husband was here to share our lives together has given me the strength to grow in such a way that this love shall not have loved in vain.

God loves you- through me and God loves me- through you!

"We are loved by God in so many different ways every day and we have our eyes closed to it.

If we stop to realize that God is the "higher person" in our being.

JUNE 19, 1979

THERE ARE MOMENTS WHEN MY SOUL FEELS THE BEAUTY OF LIFE IN ITS FULLEST AND IT IS IN THESE MOMENTS THAT GOD IS PLANTING SEEDS OF LOVE IN MY HIGHER SELF AND I LOVE IT.

AT THE TIME OF "PLANTING", MY SOUL IS CULTIVATED

AND THE SOIL OF MY SOUL IS
ENRICHED AND READY TO
RECEIVE THE "SEEDS" OF LOVE.

IT IS THE RESPONSIBILITY
OF MY LOWER SELF TO KEEP
THE CROP CULTIVATED AND
WORKED PROPERLY. IN DOING
SO, MY LOWER SELF DEVELOPS
AND BECOMES A PART OF MY
HIGHER SELF AND MY "CROP" IS
PLEASING IN THE SIGHT OF GOD.

February 11, 2000

It is time to say goodnight to another beautiful day and as I start my rituals, remove the makeup, brush my teeth etc., I see this reflection in the mirror and I am reminded that I have been blessed by having lived long enough to celebrate 78 (plus) years.

Yes, this reflection no longer has the image of the youthful complexion, or the auburn, thick silky, long hair. The slender, shapely figure that was once the image in the mirror has spread out into a more relaxed figure and the complexion too has taken on the rewards of having had the privilege of experiencing life and love these past years. My gray hair frames this face and the wrinkles, well, this is a way of

Mother Nature. I look at this figure in my mirror and I tell myself, "Would you really want to look like you were when you were young"? I guess not. So I have learned to realize that I have earned this image that I see in the mirror and I am grateful for the countless blessings that I have and I can look beyond the image in the mirror and see the essence of my being which is my soul.

This is the image that is important and shall always be beautiful in the eyes of God. God is Love and Love is Life-Life Everlasting.

It is 4 a.m. and I am moved to type this thought: on Thursday morning April 12th 2005:

I am looking at pictures of loved ones that are with me daily and I am reminded of the love they have left me with. This keeps me reliving beautiful moments that we shared together...

God is telling me that there is so much more to this love that they left us and to concentrate on the present. There is so much beauty and love with me right now that words cannot express as this love and beauty that is here with me is inexpressible. Just concentrate on the love that is, has always been and shall ever be. This takes concentration but it is there.

There is an experience that awaits all of us if we can turn our love and attention on the very present and allow this love that wants to be a part of our lives right now without reliving the past.

The past loves and memories of our loved ones is just the base for the love that surrounds us in the present. Oh! How much we have to learn about the blessings that we have and we will never be aware of the blessings of now, right now until we can go on and live and love in the present. It is true, the words that I spoke at my brother, Dale's, funeral, "These dear ones that left us so much love, we must keep it alive and pass it on."

Love never dies, it lives in all of us.

COME VISIT WITH ME

*OH! WE MET IN ANOTHER
   LIFETIME-
YOU KNOW-AS HUSBAND AND
   WIFE,
OR AS MOTHER, FATHER,
   BROTHER, SISTER, ETC.*

*THOUGHTS, YES THOUGHTS
BRING US TOGETHER, SO
BRIEFLY.*

*YOUR THOUGHTS COME TO YOU
AS YOU KNOW THEM.*

*MY (your) MEANS OF
"COMMUNICATION" CANNOT BE
REVEALED TO YOU UNTIL YOU
"LIVE" AS I DO-AFTER DEATH*

BRINGS YOU TO THIS LEVEL OF GOD'S PLAN FOR US.

WE (the deceased) ARE ALWAYS WITH YOU BUT IT IS YOU THAT MUST INVITE US TO DWELL IN YOUR EXISTENCE THAT YOU HAVEN'T LEARNED TO BE AWARE OF YET.

SO IN YOUR "QUIET TIME", (BE STILL MY HEART). LISTEN, AND YOU WILL BE ABLE TO BE WITH ME AS I AM ALWAYS WITH YOU.

GOD LEFT US WITH THE WORD, LOVE. DO WE UNDERSTAND THE DEPTH OF THE MEANING OF LOVE?

July 25, 2004

Dear God,

Once again you have given me a
chance to express my thoughts
and convictions.

So often in life we are given a
chance to change the course we
take in our daily lives.

Sometimes, it is just a kind word, or
a hug to someone who is in need.

Today, I had that happen to me
at least three times that I am
aware of.

A dear friend who just recently
discovered that she has breast
cancer and the treatment is
going to be so extensive that the
treatment is going to require a
double mastectomy.

Only she and God knows how she
   feels. Her husband is crushed
   also but his love is so supportive,
   and there too, no one knows his
   feelings but him and God.
Now, I come into the picture and I
   am so grateful and so pleased that
   she came to me for comfort and
   support.

God works in such mysterious
   ways, I am so pleased that
   God chose me to be his "go
   between" and give her comfort
   and reassurance that love for her
   is always so near. Omnipresent.
   Aren't we blessed when God
   chooses us be his messenger and
   answer prayers through us?

My second experience today is when I was driving home from church and I saw my neighbor. I stopped and told him that it was such a relief to see him as he hadn't been mowing his lawn or playing with his dog (or at least I never saw him). It is a known fact that his wife is having health problems and it is getting harder each day to meet the challenge that is required to care for her.

It was God who chose to "take the scenic view" on the way home from church. Because when I asked if there was anything that I could do to help, we agreed, that if I went walking past their house and saw her sitting in the garage, just to stop and visit with her. Perhaps she would get use to me enough that I could perhaps sit with her just long enough that he could go to the store or make short trips that just have to be done.

I did take a walk past their house tonight and they were there. He was playing with the dog and she was there sitting in the garage. She even asked me to sit next to her. We had a nice visit but it was obvious that she has a very troubled, mixed up mind.

There for the grace of God go I.

July 23, 00

9:30 pm

Early this morning, I was having a beautiful "quiet time" and these thoughts came to me:

Asking myself, "who am I, what makes me what I am?"

Going back as far as I can remember, takes me back to my very young days living on Charlevoix, in Detroit, Michigan.

There were three windows in the living room but I was too young to stand up and see over the window sill. Then --- the big moment came, for the first time, I stood up and could see outside!! What a thrill, what progress! This was such an early lesson in life that it has lasted all of these years. To discover something new.

When the time is right, we discover new things in our life, and the new discoveries become a part of our lives and remain with us for the rest of our lives.

The same with people. Going back to the time when Virginia Bennet came into my life, she always came to live with her maternal grandparents for the summer. Oh! What a good feeling it was to see Virginia and her little sister, Mary Jean, in the car, knowing that they would be there for the summer. This gave me the early lesson in appreciating friendship. It is so rewarding to have a friendship that has lasted for a life time. We have shared childhood days, playing with dolls, riding bikes, swinging on her grandmother's porch swing, watching her grandmother curl her hair around her finger and see the beautiful long curls fall into place, wishing that my straight thick hair was curly like hers. It was at her grandmother's house that introduced me to the love of good chocolate. (Her mother and two aunts worked at Crowley Milners candy kitchen.) There was always good candy in their house and at Easter time––I thought I was in Heaven showered with chocolate!!

Well as life will have it––we grew up, fell in love and got married. For reasons that I really don't understand, we went through a period in our lives when we were separated for a while.

Real friendship can live on in spite of setbacks.

We have renewed our special friendship and it is even stronger. We have laughed together, cried together, and our love has survived it all. We have lost loved ones, cried together, picked up the pieces and carried on.

Miles separate us now but that doesn't stop us from getting together when we can. And just to know that she and her David have a special place in their heart for me as I have a special place in my heart for them-is a wonderful bond for real friendship.

December 4, 2006

3 AM

I just woke up after having this dream and was inspired as this dream has such a theme for a great story.

The main character is a woman and what she did to become such a great hero is not clear.

She was in some sort of trouble and was taken away. Everyone in the town was in such an uproar that they all went to help her and when she was to "come back" everyone she was ever connected to was there and greeted her with food to share with everyone. I visioned some sort of food being cooked that seemed to be stuck together as bacon will when fried. This food was being taken apart or separated with bare hands. I noticed that they(whoever was separating it) did not wear gloves or never washed their hands and this leads me to think that there was a reason, perhaps that their help was so genuine, they wanted to give of themselves to express their joy and thanksgiving for having her back. Now-my favorite quote of Ralph Waldo Emerson's is so strong that surfaces at this time is, "No matter who you are with or for what length of time, you take something from that person and leave something of yourself with them." (I live this quote in my life and believe it strongly) Everyone that was in my dream had at one time touched the life of this "hero" and therefore was a "part of her" and she, "a part of them".

I guess the reason I was inspired so strongly to get up at this time and write this down is because it awakens me to realize that we live this process every day of our lives. But do we go out of our way to express the thanksgiving and joy of helping others and not stopping to realize that we are all a "part of each other" and we have the opportunity to help ourselves as we help others?

I am grateful for this "dream" and now I can go back to sleep feeling grateful for this "message."

Love After Death

June 15 2005 3AM

I am awake and I see Cook's picture. He was so handsome when this picture was taken and we were so in love.

Often I have wished that I had a picture of him just before he died. Because of radiation, he lost his hair and because of an accident, due to his diabetes, he lost his teeth and he lost so much weight. The tumor in his brain paralyzed his left side.

Sometimes it may take all of this to really test our love. Our love was so strong, it made us realize that it is the beautiful soul that we love and these unfortunate bouts of illness opens our "eyes" to the depth of love.

We have all heard that when we die, we take nothing with us. How wrong how very wrong. Every person that we meet, we take part of them with us and we leave part of ourselves with them. So when Cook died he never left here alone. He always saw the best in people and there was never a person that he met that didn't really admire him.

It is comforting to know that he took all of the love that I thought that I could possibly give him but there is so much more to love that we cannot understand until we die.

Just before my father died, he sat up in his death bed, his eyes opened so wide and expressed what he saw by saying,

"Everything is so beautiful, everyone should see it." Somehow these aren't the thoughts that I woke up with, but they are the thoughts that are finding themselves in print. I leave them there for tonight and go back to bed. Goodnight to all of the loved ones that have died and left me with so much of their love and took so much of my love with them.

Goodnight Sweetheart

Somehow I seem to be in a testing state. As I look back into my life with Cook, which was the Camelot of my life, there were times when I wondered if I loved him too much.

I have learned so much about loving and the difference of love of man and the love of God.

There were times in my life when I questioned myself. Would I be strong enough to choose between God and Cook? Really it was such a juvenile question as I have learned that there is no comparison to the different loves. (speaking of the mortal part of Cook) Now I can see that the real part of Cook that I loved is the Deity that lived in his body. How could I have loved a man who had Satan as his master?

Now the core of this thought is, Is my love for God strong enough that I can eventually let go of the past and the loving life that I shared with my wonderful husband, pick up the beautiful part of him that I loved so dearly, realizing that it is God that I am so in love with and find contentment once again? This is not pertaining to sex as some people may ask, not understanding my true feelings.

Sex was so beautiful and because it was so, is because it was used as a vehicle connecting the man and his soul, with the woman and her soul.

When sex is used for this purpose, how could it be anything but enjoying and together, sharing this experience with God --again another example of the holy trinity. Man-Woman- God.

Dear God,

Please keep me strong in my conviction that I may keep myself in such a way that if I am to meet another man to share this love with, it shall be beautiful because once again, it will be sharing two souls as well as two bodies. "Where two or more are gathered, there I shall be also."

COULD IT BE THAT THERE
HAS TO BE DEATH UNTIL WE
LEARN THE LESSON OF THE
ONENESS OF GOD'S SPIRIT IS
EVERYWHERE?

GOD CREATED MAN "IN HIS
OWN IMAGE" WE ARE NOT
TOLD THAT OUR IMAGE
OF GOD IS IN THE FLESH
NECESSARILY BUT IN "HIS"
IMAGE. THIS IS WHERE THE
"SPIRIT" LIES. WE ARE OF GOD'S
SPIRIT.

WHEN WE LOSE A LOVED
ONE AND FEEL THE LOSS
SO DESPERATELY, IT IS THE
MORTAL LOSS AND NOT THE

SPIRITUAL LOSS. WE ARE ONE
IN SPIRIT WITH GOD.

THROUGH THE METHOD OF
KARMA WE ARE PRIVILEGED
TO COMMUNICATE IN GOD'S
WAY WITHOUT LOVED ONES-
SPIRIT TO SPIRIT.

IN ORDER TO UNDERSTAND
THIS WE FIRST HAVE TO
BE AWARE OF GOD'S SPIRIT
WITHIN OURSELVES AND THE
SAME SPIRIT THAT THE BODY
OF OUR LOVED ONES HOUSED.

THIS IS NOT EASY, OUR HEARTS
STILL BREAK AND OUR LIVES
SEEM TO GO ON WITH OUT

MEANING WHEN WE ARE
SEPERATED FROM OUR LOVED
ONES.

NOW THIS IS THE THOUGHT
THAT COMES TO ME IN THIS
LESSON–

WHY DO WE HAVE TO GO
THROUGH THE TRIAL OF BIRTH
AND DEATH IF IT IS THE SPIRIT
THAT IS THE ONLY LIVING PART
OF US THAT IS ETERNAL?

WHEN WE LEARN THE LESSON
THAT WE MUST LEARN, TO
BECOME MORE AWARE OF
THE "SPIRIT" AND LIVE SUCH
A LIFE THAT THE SPIRIT WILL

BE THE MASTER AND NOT THE
MORTAL BODY THAT MUST BE
SHED?

I PRAY TO GOD THAT I MAY
BECOME MORE FAMILIAR
WITH GOD'S SPIRIT THAT
LIVES WITHIN MY BODY AND
ACCEPTING THE FACT THAT
THIS SAME ONENESS WITH GOD
WAS, IS, AND SHALL ALWAYS BE,
THE REASON FOR MY LOVING
THE LOVE THAT HAS BEEN
TAKEN FROM ME.

IT IS SUCH A HARD LESSON TO
GO ON IN LIFE WITHOUT MY
DEAR HUSBAND. HOW MANY
PEOPLE HAVE GONE THROUGH

THIS TRIAL-AND HOW MANY
WILL HAVE TO FACE IT IN THEIR
LIFE TIME?

WHAT IS THIS LESSON THAT
MANKIND MUST LEARN? WE
WILL GO ON HURTING AND
SUFFERING UNTIL WE CAN
OPEN OUR HEARTS, MINDS
AND SOULS TO GOD AND
SIMPLY ACCEPT HIS ORIGINAL
PLAN FOR US. JUST TO ACCEPT
"HIS" LOVE COMPLETELY,
WHEN MANKIND CAN DO
THIS WITHOUT RESERVATION-
COULD IT BE, THERE WILL
NO LONGER BE DEATH
AS WE KNOW IT, BUT LIFE
EVERLASTING?

A Quiet Time With God

As I get into my bed at night, I find myself
  saying,
"Dear God, it is just You and me and here I
  am without reservations.
Please use me.
And if tomorrow, you need me to do some
  chore, thought or deed, it will be my
  pleasure to do Thy will.
Just program me now, as I lie still.
And if tomorrow, if things happen that I
  don't understand, help me to remember
  and listen when you tell me, "Oh! yes
  you can".
Or if life chooses to grant me bliss,---
please don't let me forget--You gave me this.!!
So goodnight, my Dearest Friend, thanks for
  today, for using me.
Thanks for the privilege of letting me see,-

It's not my will, but Thine be done. And in
the end, I know that You have won."

Amen

WORDS FAIL ME!

IF I COULD WRITE TO YOU,
THE WORDS I'D LIKE TO SAY.
I'D WRITE THE THOUGHTS
I SHARE WITH GOD,
AS I KNEEL AT NIGHT TO PRAY

BUT THOUGHTS ARE
    THOUGHTS
AND WORDS ARE WORDS,
AND TOGETHER THEY CAN'T
    EXPRESS,
THE LOVE FOR YOU THAT'S IN
    MY HEART.
--I WISH YOU THE VERY BEST.

Sunset/Sunrise

As sure as we open our eyes
  and see,
the sun setting in the West,
we are aware of the beautiful
  colors.
The red, blue, green, yellow,
  orange and lavender.

Let us keep these colors vivid in
  our mind.
And transpose them to be an aura
  that completely surrounds us.

The feeling is so beautiful, I feel a
  smile forming from within and it
  is visible on my face.

As my day is ending, I ask God to
  kindle my awareness of the sunset

of this day in my life and as I go
to rest, I take with me, its beauty.

While my body "sleeps" and my
soul is in close communion with
God during the night, how else
but beautiful can tomorrow be?

Surely, every sunrise is no contest
in comparison to any sunset!!

In the night, all is quiet--
My body goes to rest.
It seems my soul-
goes to God---
Like a bird goes to its nest.

This Moment

This moment was worth waiting for.

This moment, not an hour ago or
even five minutes ago, but, "This
Moment."

Everything is so beautiful-so right, don't
think about five minutes from now
but just appreciate "This Moment"

There are times when life is challenging.

You may feel lonely, misunderstood,
rejected or perhaps even wonder what
life is all about.

Just remember the God given
"moments" when you can enjoy a
beautiful sunset or when the sun
breaks the darkness of night time and
a new day is born.

Know that you are someone special.
There is no one that can replace you.

When you walk on the beach and see
your footprints in the wet sand and
the tide comes up and washes them
back into the sea----- you have
left your "mark" that no one can
duplicate. This is your "moment".
Each "moment" has a special meaning
for us in our lifetime. If we stop
and count the blessings that "one
moment" brings to us, our life will be
indelible on the pages of history that
will be omnipresent.

Enjoy "This Moment" as only you can.

Weeds In The Garden Of Life

Why do weeds grow so abundantly in a
garden that we care for so tenderly?

Weeds grow so fast and choke the life of
flowers planted as Man and Wife.

The weeds of life grow everywhere, without
feeling, without care.

To be a gardener of life, we must be strong,
to tend the good and weed the wrong.

Plant your garden carefully, and plant it in
a row.
Watch your garden faithfully-
keep it in control.

In between and out of sight,
weeds are strong with untold might.
so busy in the sunshine and asleep at night.

The gardens that were planted for us
need constant care.
All of this beauty is ours-
to love and to share.

Don't let your garden grow in clay,
Till the rich soil and
"weed" it every day.

When Life Seems Hard

God never intended for these things to
   happen.
This wasn't His plan at all!

Why did man spoil the beauty of life?
Why did man turn ugly and fall?

Why can't we accept each other and try
   to get along?
There are days when nothing seems
   right,
Everything we do or say, --is wrong!

To think highly of one's self and
   remember,
God is our Friend.
To try our very best, and trust-----
this ugliness------will end!

To end a day in this state of mind
wasn't God's plan at all.
To see His Own turn from Grace and
helplessly watch him fall.

How fortunate I am to have God as my
friend.
He helps me to pick up the pieces, and
tomorrow,--
I'll try again!!

GOD'S ALWAYS THERE

THE CLOUDS ARE DARK AND
  GLOOMY,
THERE IS SADNESS IN THE AIR.
MY HEART IS SORE WITH
  SADNESS
AND I WONDER, GOD,
DON'T YOU CARE?

HOW MUCH MORE IS COMING?
HOW MUCH CAN I BEAR?
DON'T YOU HEAR ME
  CALLING, GOD?
ARE YOU THERE?

MY WORLD IS FAILING ME
AND I AM HELPLESS IN ITS
  MIDST.
THE WEIGHT IS CRUSHING
  UPON ME

AND I FEEL BURIED IN ITS PITS.

I HEAR "READ PSALM 77 AND
HEAR ME WHEN I SAY,
YOU ARE THE PSALMS OF
   YESTERDAY AND YES, I HEAR
   YOU WHEN I PRAY!

"I HEARD YOU SCREAM AND
   WONDER,
I UNDERSTOOD YOU IN
   DESPAIR.
I WATCHED AND WAITED
   PATIENTLY,
AND YES, I AM ALWAYS THERE.

"IT IS JUST AS I HAVE PROMISED,
MY WORD IS STRONG AND
   TRUE.

YOU DON'T HAVE TO SCREAM
   FOR HELP--
I AM PATIENTLY WAITING
   FOR YOU.

"MY HEART IS ALSO HEAVY,
MY BLOOD I SHED FOR YOU.
CAN'T YOU HEAR MY CRIES OF
   PAIN
WHEN I CALL OUT TO YOU?

"I MADE YOU IN MY OWN
   IMAGE,
HOW MUCH MORE COULD I
   CARE?
DON'T YOU THINK I HAVE
   FEELINGS,
WHEN YOU ARE IN DESPAIR?

"MY ARMS ARE OPEN AND MY
   HEART
ACHES FOR YOUR EMBRACE.
ALL DARK CLOUDS SHALL PASS
   AWAY,
AND A RAINBOW WILL TAKE ITS
   PLACE."

Yesterday, Today. Forever

What happened today that changed my
    life?
Write poetry and what does it say?

Does it speak of events or weather in an
    unusual way?

We write about life in a subconscious
    state of mind and what we write
    down, becomes history in time.

We write about books we read,
    songs we sing or perhaps we see an
    interesting play.

The events that mold our life,
----------- just history today.

Five years from now or even ten,
we can read this poem-----------
just history again.

I'M DYING

I'm dying, just waiting to start anew.
But as I stand here-so naked
my branches so brittle and my
leaves shed with my youth.
I'll wait a little while as I
have a message for you.
Efrain, you have been such
a friend to me and
shared my youthful years.
Now that I'm old you understand and
shed some mourning tears.
When you look at my naked body its
silhouette in the sky.
You see me in my youthful years
and you don't want me to die.
But my dear friend Efrain, I've watched
you grow some too and it gives
me pleasure to know you care and
Efrain, *I love you too.*

Written for Efrain Perez

MY QUIET PLACE

WHEN I GO OFF TO MY QUIET
*   PLACE*
AND LEAVE MY BODY BEHIND,
SUCH PEACE AND TRANQUILITY
ON EARTH, I CANNOT FIND.

A PLACE WHERE ONLY GOD
*   CAN GO,*
AND HE TAKES ME BY MY HAND
HE LEADS ME THERE TO BE
*   WITH HIM*
AND THIS, I SURELY KNOW.

HE GIVES ME THOUGHTS, AND
*   LOVING WORDS*
AND TELLS ME, "PEN THESE
*   DOWN."*
I HAVE NO IDEA, WHAT THESE
*   WORDS WILL BE,*

BUT "THEY"' JUST COME
   AROUND.

I WAKE UP IN THE ODDEST
   HOURS
WITH THESE THOUGHTS GOING
   THROUGH MY MIND.
IT IS SUCH A PEACEFUL
   FEELING,
IN THIS "QUIET PLACE" OF
   MINE.

DEPTH OF LOVE

I PRAY IT IS NOT MY LIPS YOU
    ARE KISSING,
NOR MY "BODY" IN YOUR
    ARMS.
BUT WHEN OUR LIPS ARE
    MEETING,
IT IS MY SOUL THAT HOLDS
    YOUR CHARM.

AND WHEN YOUR ARMS
    ENFOLD ME
AND YOU WHISPER IN MY EAR,
"I LOVE YOU, NOW AND
    FOREVER,"
IT IS YOUR SOUL I SEE AND
    HEAR.

WHEN TWO HEARTS ARE
    MARRIED,

AND TWO SOULS ARE AS ONE,
GOD HAS BLESSED THIS
   MARRIAGE
AND **HE** WHISPERS, "THIS WELL
   DONE!"

IT IS NOT LOVE OF A PASSION
THAT I SEEK WITHIN YOUR
   TOUCH,
BUT THE LOVE OF YOU, THE
   TOUCH OF YOU,
THE DEPTH OF YOU, THE "YOU"
   I LOVE SO MUCH!

THERE IS A WALL WITHIN OUR
   WORLD,
IF ONLY I COULD CLIMB.
FOR ON THE OTHER SIDE IS A
   PART OF YOU

THAT I AM TRYING TO FIND!

A PART OF YOU THAT I COULD
   LOVE
AS MUCH AS I LOVE YOU NOW,
IF ONLY YOU WOULD BREAK
   DOWN THIS WALL
AND LET ME LOVE THE "ALL"
   OF YOU--
IF ONLY I KNEW HOW!!!

IF THERE IS A PART OF ME YOU
   CANNOT SEE,
JUST LET ME KNOW SOMEHOW.
FOR WHEN I GIVE MY LOVE
   TO YOU,
I GIVE IT ALL--RIGHT NOW.
(AND I DO LOVE YOU. "NOW
   AND FOREVER.")

WELL, THERE WERE MORE
  CHRISTMAS BALLS,
BEADS OF GLASS,
BELLS IN CERAMIC, AND IN
  STRAW.
I HUNG THEM ALL.
THEN STOOD BACK AND
  LOOKED AT THEM
IN AWE!
THANKS MOM, FOR ALL THE
  CHRISTMASES PAST.
EVEN FOR THE DOLLS WITH
  HAIR,
THAT I HAVE LEARNED TO
  LOVE AT LAST.

IT IS CHRISTMAS TIME AGAIN,
AND THOUGH WE ARE MILES
  APART

WE WILL BE TOGETHER
  CHRISTMAS MORN,
AS WE LIVE IN EACH OTHER'S
  HEART.

MERRY CHRISTMAS TO
  MY MOM,
AND TO HER HUSBAND, SAM.
TOGETHER LET'S MAKE THIS
  YEAR AHEAD
AS HAPPY AS WE CAN.

P.S. I LOVE YOU.

To Norma from Cook.

LOVE SHALL FIND ITS WAY
ON THIS MORNING IN MY NEW
   LIFE.
I THANK GOD FOR YOU--MY
   WIFE.

TO START THIS DAY AS "ONE"
   WITH YOU,
I PLIGHT MY LOVE TO KEEP IT
   TRUE.

LIKE A BRAND NEW DAY AND
   THE MORNING SUN.
OUR LIFE TOGETHER HAS JUST
   BEGUN.

THERE'LL BE MOMENTS THAT
   AREN'T SO KIND,

BUT I'LL HOLD YOUR HAND--
   YOU HOLD MINE,
AND LOVE SHALL FIND ITS WAY.

(LOVE GROWS FROM UP AND
   DOWN,
MORE LAUGHTER THAN TEARS,
MORE SMILES THAN FROWNS.)

I THOUGHT OF MASTERPIECES
    YESTERDAY
AND I LET THEM SLIP AWAY.
THESE GOD GIVEN THOUGHTS
WERE MEANT TO SHARE!
TO BE WRITTEN DOWN FOR
    THOSE WHO CARE.

TO START A DAY IN SOLITUDE,
TO TASTE THE DAWN, AS DAILY
    FOOD.

TO HEAR A BIRD AS IT SINGS
TO WATCH THE GRACE OF FLIGHT
AS IT SPREADS ITS WINGS!

A PETUNIA AWAKENS AND
    SMILES AT THEE,
THESE ARE THE THINGS WE
    ARE ALLOWED TO SEE.

TO FEEL THE BREEZE UPON
   YOUR FACE
AND TO KNOW THIS IS GOD'S
   GENTLE EMBRACE.

THE BEAUTY AND WARMTH OF
   THE RISING SUN,
WHAT A WELCOME FOR A DAY
   THAT'S JUST BEGUN.

GOD'S BLESSINGS ARE SO
   ABUNDANTLY WAITING
OH GOD WHAT BEAUTY YOU
   HAD FOR ME THIS DAY.
IN THE STILL OF THE MORNING,
   I WAS
BUT SOFT WILLING CLAY.

AND AS THE DAY UNFOLDED

AND YOUR BLESSINGS
TO UNFOLD
LEFT ME WITH TREASURES
    THAT I FEEL
MUST BE TOLD!

THE ESSENSE OF LOVE THAT
    WAS EXPRESSED,
LEFT ME WITH RAPTURE AND
    FILLED MY BREAST.

THE FAMILY TIES THAT ARE
    TRUE AND STRONG
WERE PROVEN RIGHT-
THERE IS NO WRONG!

I GIVE THANKS FOR FRIENDS SO
    TRUE
AND FAMILY-DEAR,

THEY COME FROM YOU.

IF A LESSON TODAY I HAVE
    LEARNED,
THANK YOU, GOD, FOR EVENTS
    THAT TURN.

FROM SADNESS AND FORLORN
TO THANKSGIVING
AND THE BEAUTY OF EACH
    NEW MORN.

NOW IT IS NIGHT -THIS DAY IS
    'ORE
AND I GO TO SLEEP-NO LONGER
    POOR.

Thank you God
for all your blessings!